TRUCKS

IAN GRAHAM

This edition produced in **1995** for
Shooting Star Press Inc
Suite 1212
230 Fifth Avenue
New York, NY 10001

© Aladdin Books Ltd 1990

Created and produced by
Aladdin Books
28 Percy Street
London, W1P 9FF

*First published in the
United States in 1991 by*
Gloucester Press

Design David West
Children's Book Design

Editorial Lionheart Books

Researcher Cecilia Weston-Baker

Illustrator Aziz Khan
and Ron Hayward

ISBN 1-57335-164-4

Printed in Belgium

CONTENTS

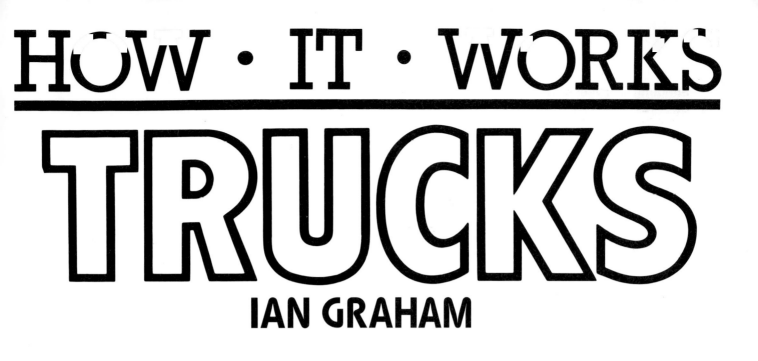

HOW · IT · WORKS

TRUCKS

IAN GRAHAM

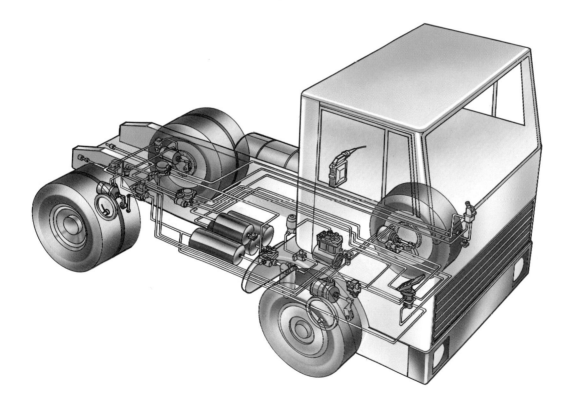

SHOOTING STAR PRESS

WORKING PARTS

A truck is a motor vehicle designed to transport heavy goods. The tractor unit at the front of the truck shown here contains the engine and the driver's cab. Behind it, a platform or trailer carries the cargo or load.

Most trucks are powered by diesel engines, because they are more powerful than an equivalent gasoline-fueled engine. The diesel fuel they use is also less expensive than gasoline. Engine power may be boosted by the addition of a turbocharger to increase the pressure inside the engine.

Trucks use many of the same kinds of parts as cars or any other road vehicles. However, because a truck carries heavy loads, its basic framework, called its chassis, must be much stronger than a car's chassis. Its engine must be more powerful than a car's and its brakes must be able to stop the truck safely with its maximum load on board. Its wheels and tires must be able to support the weight of the heaviest load it can carry. A truck usually has many more wheels than a car in order to evenly distribute the weight of its load. The springs in its suspension system must be much sturdier than a car's to provide a smooth ride over a bumpy road surface.

Today, most goods carried by trucks are either packed into standard sized containers or tied on to standard wooden platforms that are called pallets. Pallets are specially designed to be lifted and moved by powerful vehicles called forklifts.

The shape of a truck is important in keeping down fuel costs. A lumpy,

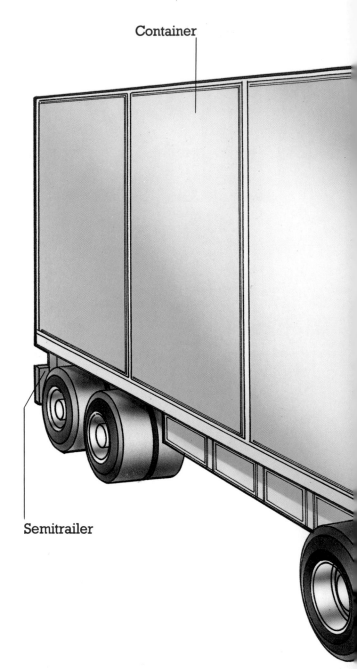

Container

Semitrailer

angular load can increase a truck's air resistance, slowing it down and resulting in more fuel being burned to overcome that effect. By packing the load inside smooth-sided containers or covering it with smooth plastic sheets, air resistance is minimized. The driver's cab may also have rounded contours and a specially shaped roof to direct air smoothly over the top of the load and reduce air resistance.

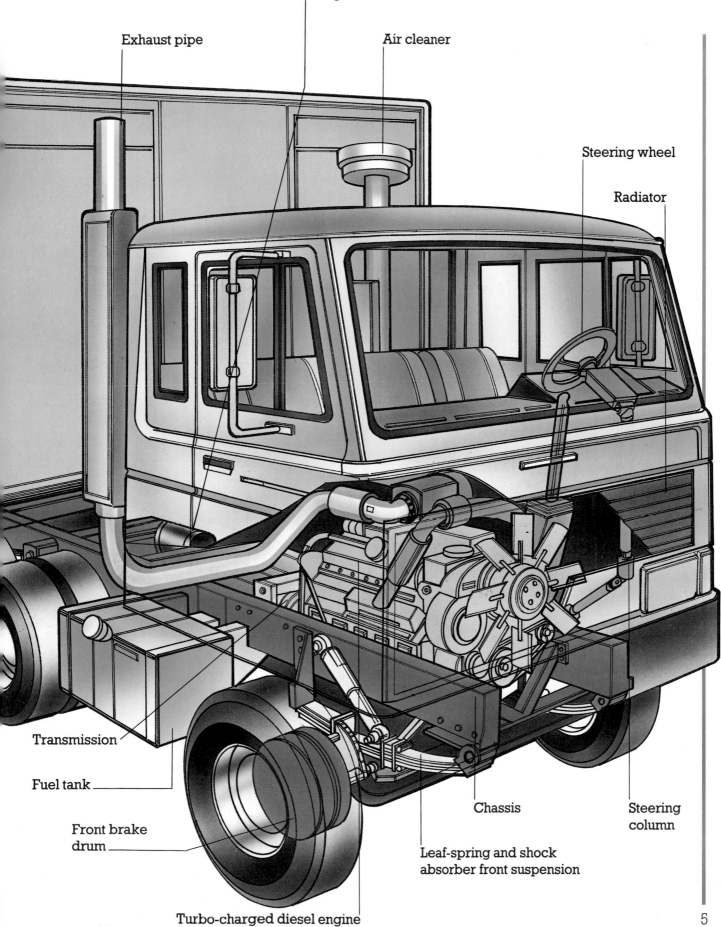

Compressed air tanks

Exhaust pipe

Air cleaner

Steering wheel

Radiator

Transmission

Fuel tank

Front brake drum

Chassis

Steering column

Leaf-spring and shock absorber front suspension

Turbo-charged diesel engine

5

DIFFERENT TYPES

There are many different shapes and sizes of trucks used for a wide variety of tasks, but all of them can be divided into two types, called rigid (or straight) and articulated.

The driver's cab and the body of a rigid truck are firmly attached to the same framework, called a chassis. An articulated truck has two parts, a tractor unit and a load-carrying trailer, which are linked together by a pivot called the fifth wheel. This allows the truck to bend in the middle and turn corners more easily. As an articulated truck's trailer has road wheels only at the rear, and its front end is supported by the tractor unit, its correct name is a semitrailer.

An articulated truck can detach its tractor from one semitrailer and hook it up to another semitrailer. This saves time because the tractor need not wait for a trailer to be loaded or unloaded before it can continue working. Without the tractor, the front of the semitrailer is supported by small wheels on legs which can be jacked up and down when necessary. The tractor is backed on to the semitrailer once it is loaded.

An articulated truck from the United States.

An American car-breakdown and recovery truck.

A rigid truck.

A British cab-over truck.

DIESEL ENGINE

Modern trucks are fitted with diesel engines. These are similar to the type of gasoline engine used by most cars. Both use pistons to convert the energy stored in the fuel into mechanical power to turn the wheels. They use different fuels. Most cars use gasoline. Diesel engines use a heavier fuel called diesel oil, which in Britain is also called DERV (Diesel Engine Road Vehicle).

The fuel is burned in different ways in the two types of engines. In a gasoline engine, a fine mist of the fuel is sucked into each cylinder. The mixture of fuel droplets and air is compressed by a piston and then ignited by an electric

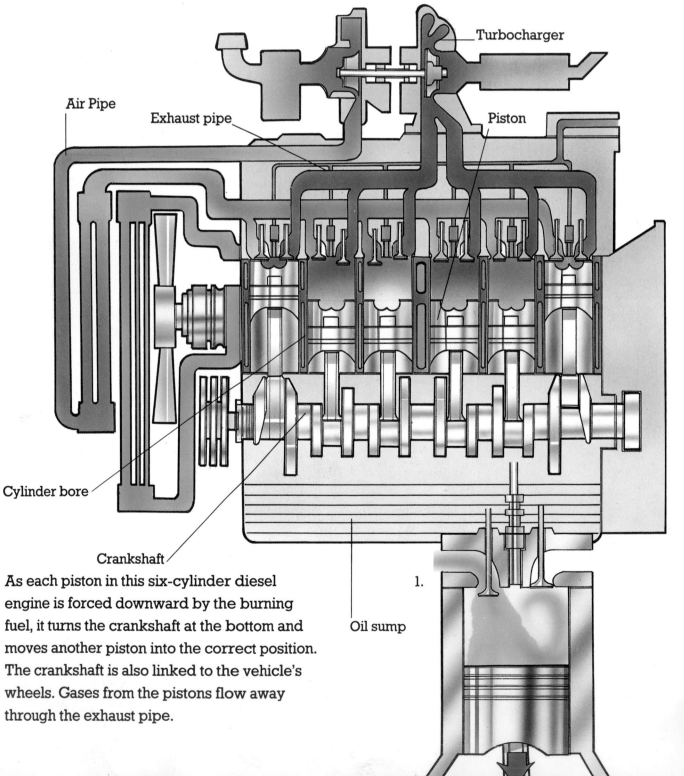

Turbocharger

Air Pipe

Exhaust pipe

Piston

Cylinder bore

Crankshaft

1.

Oil sump

As each piston in this six-cylinder diesel engine is forced downward by the burning fuel, it turns the crankshaft at the bottom and moves another piston into the correct position. The crankshaft is also linked to the vehicle's wheels. Gases from the pistons flow away through the exhaust pipe.

Turbocharger

Before fuel will burn, it must be mixed with air. Without the oxygen in the air, burning cannot take place. All engines suck in air from the atmosphere for this purpose. If more oxygen were available, the fuel would burn more efficiently and the engine would be more powerful. A turbocharger achieves this by compressing the incoming air before it reaches the cylinders where it is compressed again by the pistons.

The propeller-like turbine that compresses the air is powered by a second turbine. This is driven by the hot exhaust gases that rush out of the engine. Some ordinary family station wagons are now fitted with turbochargers similar to those used in trucks.

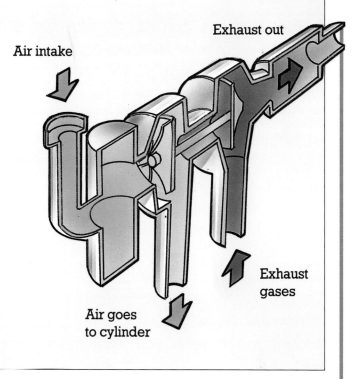

Air intake

Exhaust out

Exhaust gases

Air goes to cylinder

spark. This is called spark ignition. In a diesel engine, air is sucked into each cylinder and compressed. Squeezing the air into a much smaller space like this heats it to over 930°F. When the diesel fuel is sprayed into the cylinder at this temperature, it ignites and burns without the need for a spark. This is called compression ignition.

The four-stroke cycle. On the intake stroke (1), the falling piston reduces pressure in the cylinder, sucking in air through the inlet valve. The piston rises, compressing the air (2). The exhaust valve is closed, preventing the air escaping. Fuel sprayed into the hot air burns, expands and drives the piston downward (3). The piston rises again and pushes waste gases out through the exhaust valve (4).

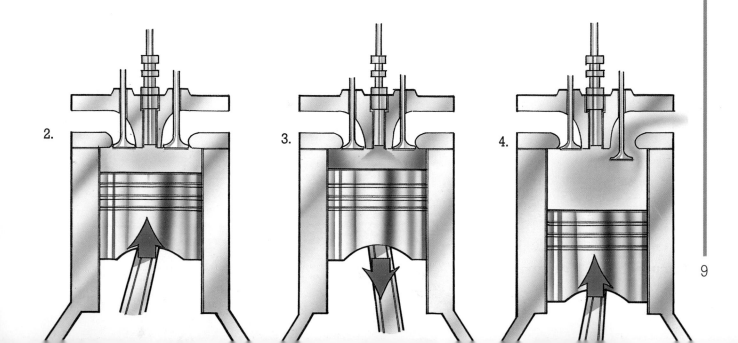

2.

3.

4.

WHEELS AND SUSPENSION

A truck's wheels and suspension system serve several important purposes: they support the weight of the truck; the wheels and tires transmit the power of the engine to the road; and the suspension system smooths out bumps in the road that could make the truck difficult to handle, uncomfortable to drive, and damage a delicate load.

The oldest type of suspension system uses springs. If the truck drives over a bump, the wheel bounces up over it. This compresses the leaf- (not a coiled) spring above the wheel, preventing the violent movement from reaching the rest of the truck. Most trucks still use spring suspension.

A newer type of suspension system uses "air springs." The front of the truck has normal metal springs, but the rear is supported by a special air suspension system.

Air springs are bags filled with air, like a football. If the truck hits a bump in the road, the bag is flattened slightly as the air is compressed. Then it bounces back to its original shape. Dump trucks that ride over rough ground may also be fitted with solid rubber springs.

Suspension

Air suspensions are beginning to replace metal spring systems. Some air suspensions can be pumped up or down to raise or lower the truck for easier loading. Metal springs are also beginning to be replaced by composite springs. Composites are plastic and glass fiber materials that are lightweight and also extremely strong.

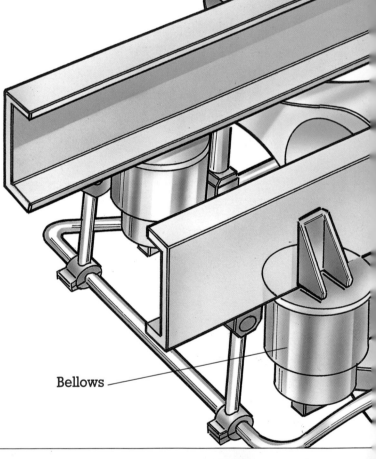

Bellows

Wheel layouts

Trucks are classified not only by whether they are articulated or rigid, but also by their wheel arrangement. Tractor units may have four or six wheels with two-, four- or six-wheel drive. Trailers may have wheels on one, two or three axles. In some countries, more than one trailer may be pulled by a tractor to form what is popularly called a road-train.

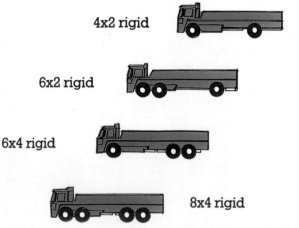

4x2 rigid

6x2 rigid

6x4 rigid

8x4 rigid

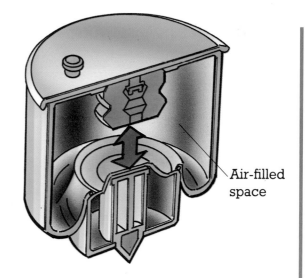

Bellows

The air-filled bags used in air suspensions are called bellows. The air pressure inside the bellows controls the system's performance.

Air-filled space

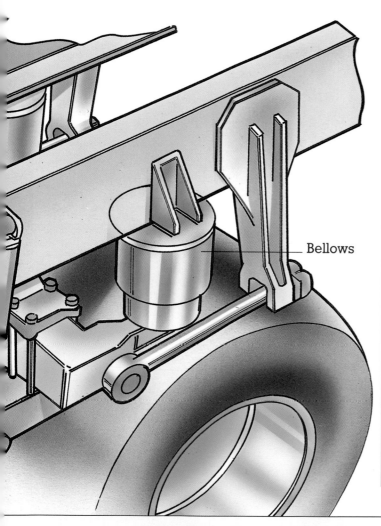

Bellows

Part of a leaf-spring on a truck.

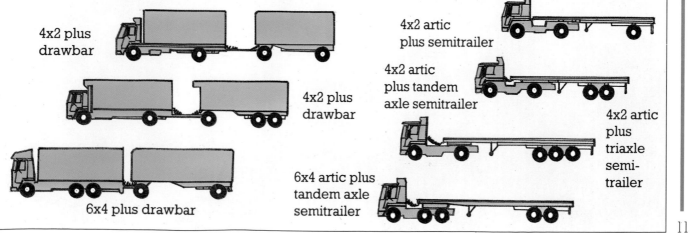

4x2 plus drawbar

4x2 plus drawbar

6x4 plus drawbar

6x4 artic plus tandem axle semitrailer

4x2 artic plus semitrailer

4x2 artic plus tandem axle semitrailer

4x2 artic plus triaxle semi-trailer

BRAKES

Trucks have the most complex braking systems found on any vehicles. Air brakes, or full-air, are the most common. The truck's engine drives an air compressor. High pressure air from the compressor is sent to a tank called a reservoir, where it is kept until needed. When the driver presses the brake pedal on the cab floor, valves open and allow the air to flow from the reservoir along pipes, or "air lines," to the wheels.

At each wheel, the high pressure air pushes against a flexible diaphragm. This moves a push-rod, which forces brake shoes against the brake drum. The brake drum revolves along with the wheel. When the brake shoes are forced against it, the wheel stops.

In the past, if a truck's air brakes lost air pressure for any reason, the brakes failed and the truck could not be stopped. Trucks now have secondary braking systems which prevent a total loss of brakes. They also have spring brakes where the vehicle's air system holds off the brake. In the event of a total loss of air the spring brake is released and the brakes come on.

Coiled air lines carry air from the cab to operate the trailer's air brakes.

Brake shoes are coated with a material that wears away very slowly. Every time the brakes are operated, a little more of the shoe's coating is rubbed away. The brakes must be examined from time to time to ensure that they still have a safe thickness of this coating. When this becomes too thin, the brake shoes must be replaced. Springs that pull the shoes away from the drum when the brake is released may also need replacing.

A truck's disk brake.

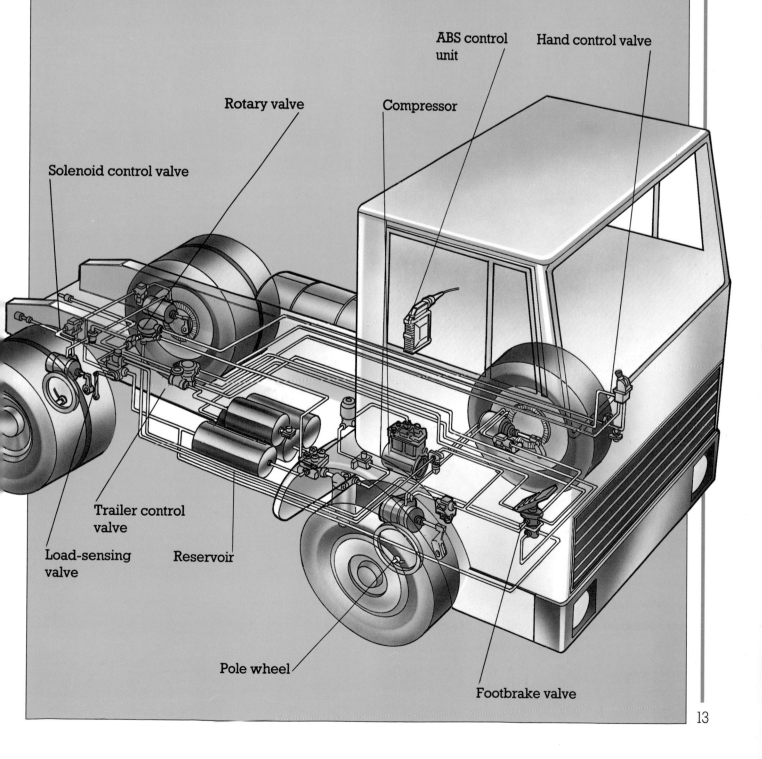

Solenoid control valve

Rotary valve

ABS control unit

Compressor

Hand control valve

Trailer control valve

Load-sensing valve

Reservoir

Pole wheel

Footbrake valve

THE DRIVER'S CABIN

The cabin, or cab, of a truck is the driver's workplace. It must be comfortable because the driver will be at the wheel for hours at a time. The position and height of the driver's seat must be adjustable to suit the individual shape and requirements of each driver. With a badly adjusted seat, the driver could get severe backache. A large windshield and the high-up position of the cabin give the driver an excellent view of the road ahead.

Long-distance drivers can be away from base with their trucks for weeks. A bed is usually built into the back of the cab so that the driver can sleep in the truck by the roadside. Some also have a television set for the driver's off-duty entertainment.

Many truck drivers now have a two-way radio in the cab. The Citizen's Band, or CB, Radio originated in the United States. It is used to contact other truck drivers or to call for assistance if there is a problem.

The tachograph

In the 1960s and 1970s there was increasing concern about the long hours that some truck drivers were working. They were becoming overtired, and this could be dangerous if they lost control of their vehicles.

Driving hours could be controlled only if there was some way of checking them. The answer was the tachograph, introduced at the end of the 1970s. It is a device that produces a trace on paper showing a driver's working hours and vehicle operations. It was an unwelcome device and was nicknamed "the spy in the cab."

A driver contacts fellow truckers by radio.

The speedometer in a driver's cab.

The cab of a modern truck is spacious and comfortable. The air temperature is controlled by a heating unit (10). All the controls (1-3) are situated within easy reach of the driver. All the dials and indicators (11-14) are positioned so that they can be seen clearly. Washers and wipers (7) keep the windshield clean. Mirrors (6,8) give the driver a clear view of the trailer, and of the road behind the truck. On many modern trucks there are computerized instrument systems that warn the driver of any vehicle faults, and monitor the efficiency of the engine. This helps to keep down the maintenance, servicing and repair costs.

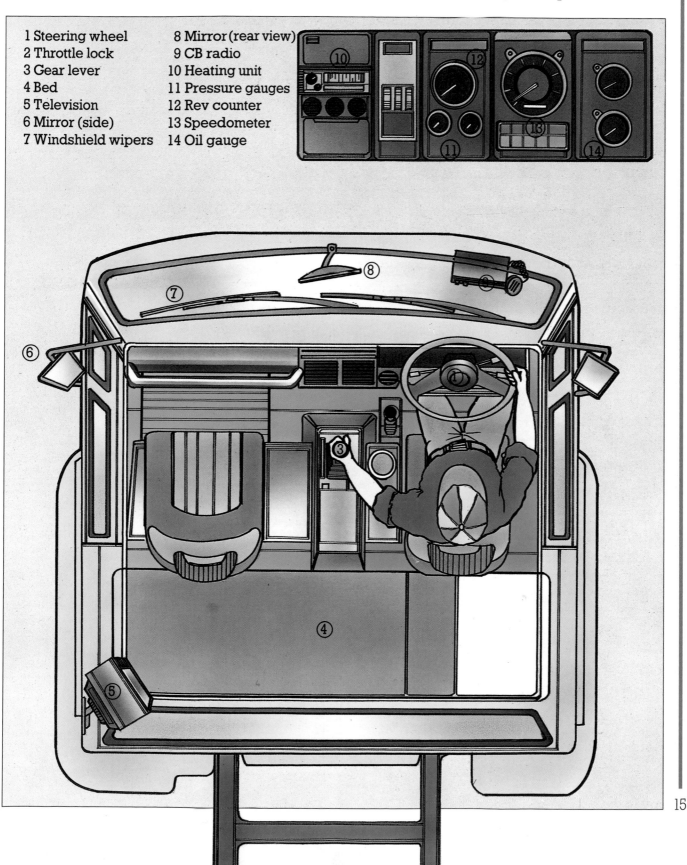

1 Steering wheel
2 Throttle lock
3 Gear lever
4 Bed
5 Television
6 Mirror (side)
7 Windshield wipers
8 Mirror (rear view)
9 CB radio
10 Heating unit
11 Pressure gauges
12 Rev counter
13 Speedometer
14 Oil gauge

VARIOUS LOADS

Trucks carry a wide variety of loads. A truck may pull a simple platform on which goods are stacked, but many trucks are specially designed for a particular type of load. Dump trucks are designed to carry loose materials such as gravel or rock. The trailers of some trucks are refrigerated so that foods such as raw meat or fish can be kept cold. Liquids ranging from gasoline to milk are transported in tankers, some of which are refrigerated.

The majority of trucks carry either solid goods or liquids, but not both. However, there are a few combination trucks that can carry all kinds of materials at the same time. They look like normal freight trucks. The difference is that they have "belly tanks" under the trailer floor that can be filled with a liquid load. They were first used in the 1950s, but were not successful because of their great weight. Now, lighter materials mean that these combination trucks can be built successfully.

Some jobs cannot be done by a general-purpose transporter. A specially designed truck, for example a garbage lorry or tanker, is vital in a wide range of situations.

A garbage truck.

Freezer trucks enable frozen foods to be transported at sub-zero temperatures.

A "wrecker" recovers crashed or broken-down cars.

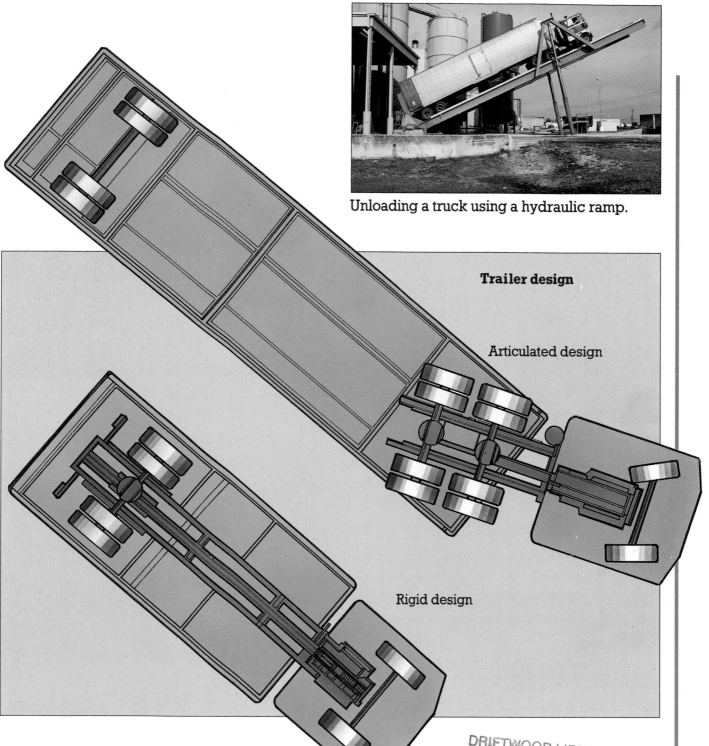

Unloading a truck using a hydraulic ramp.

Trailer design

Articulated design

Rigid design

Liquids are transported in bulk by tankers.

A car has two tires per axle, but a truck may have more. The weight that each wheel supports can be reduced by fitting more than two wheels to an axle. Many trucks also have more than two axles. Increasing the area of rubber on the road also improves traction and braking performance.

17

LOADING UP

All trucks have to be loaded and then unloaded. Until the 1960s, many drivers were responsible for doing these jobs themselves. Since that time, loading machinery has been introduced for almost all materials and freight.

Trucks that deliver bricks to building sites, for example, usually have a small hydraulic hoist built into the truck for lifting piles of bricks onto the truck and off again. Standard freight containers are frequently so heavy that they can only be loaded onto trucks by crane.

Smaller trucks used for delivering goods such as washing machines may have a tailgate lift. This is a motorized platform that folds out from the back of the truck. It can be raised or lowered simply by pressing a switch within reach of the tailgate. A delivery is slid out onto the lift, which is then lowered to the ground. A number of goods are transported on wooden platforms called pallets. These are moved around freight yards and loaded on to transporters by forklift trucks.

Loading a car transporter

First, the top deck of a car transporter is lowered on hydraulic rams, and the cars are driven on. Each car is locked securely in place by chains. When the top deck is full, it is raised and the lower deck is loaded in the same way.

A tailgate lift makes loading easier.

A logger has its own hydraulic crane.

A container truck being loaded by crane.

The tractor of an articulated truck and its semitrailer are linked by a device called the fifth wheel. One half of it is a circular plate and locking mechanism fitted to the tractor. The other half is a large pin on the semitrailer. When the cab reverses toward the semitrailer, the two halves lock together. Articulated trucks are highly maneuverable. They can turn tighter corners than rigid trucks and be driven through quite narrow gaps. To negotiate a tight corner, the tractor swings out wide and drives far forward, then turns sharply.

An articulated truck's fifth wheel.

HEAVY LOADS

In the construction industry, heavy loads frequently need to be moved from one place to another by road. Thousands of tons of earth may have to be dug out and removed to make way for the foundations of a new highway. Cranes and pile-driving equipment may have to be brought to the site by road. Building materials must be transported from their manufacturers to building sites that are perhaps several hundred miles away. When a power station or oil refinery is being built, most parts are constructed on site, but some of them must be manufactured elsewhere, and transported to the site by road. At airports, the world's biggest passenger jets are moved around on the ground near the terminals by small, yet very powerful trucks.

Australian road trains are among the world's biggest trucks.

Military trucks also have to cope with heavy loads. Tanks, for example, which are so heavy that their tracks can damage the road surface – the British Challenger main battle tank can weigh up to 62 tons. Also, tanks sometimes deteriorate around their base and have to be brought in for repairs. When they have to be transported by road, they are carried on top of purpose-built tank transporters.

An especially long articulated truck.

Large passenger aircraft are moved around airports, fueled and loaded by a fleet of specially designed vehicles. The tiny trucks, that move aircraft around have very powerful engines and are called tugs (above) after the tugboats that pull huge ocean-going ships in and out of harbors. They are built low and flat so that they can be driven around underneath the aircraft's wings without causing any damage.

The first American Space Shuttle Orbiter was transported by truck on one occasion. In 1977, the spacecraft was pulled 25 miles from its assembly site to the launch pad. The truck used was capable of pulling over 500 tons.

OFF-ROAD SPECIALS

The majority of trucks carry loads by road, but in some cases trucks must be able to travel where there are no roads. A truck specially designed for this is called an off-road vehicle. It may have all-wheel drive – that is, all the wheels are connected to the engine and are driven by it. There may also be a separate suspension system for each wheel, called independent suspension, because off-road vehicles may have to travel across very bumpy ground. Independent suspension gives a smoother ride than the suspension system fitted to road vehicles.

There are different types of off-road vehicles, each designed to do a particular job. The construction industry uses many of them. Small dump trucks transport rocks, gravel, sand or dirt around building sites. Giant dump trucks move hundreds of tons of rock and soil from earthworks in each load.

Military off-road vehicles are used to transport troops and equipment over rough or muddy ground. They also carry cranes, help build bridges, and rescue broken-down tanks and other vehicles. Some are amphibious – they can float and propel themselves through water, as well as ride over rough ground.

A military off-road vehicle.

A back-up truck used in the Paris-Dakar car rally.

The Terex Titan can transport loads weighing up to 550 tons.

Snow wheels

Even the special tires that off-road vehicles use have difficulty in gripping a surface covered with snow or ice. In countries where snow and icy conditions are common, trucks are frequently equipped with snow chains. These are designed to bite into the surface and improve grip.

Wide tyres are used in arctic conditions.

Chains in place on truck wheel give extra grip.

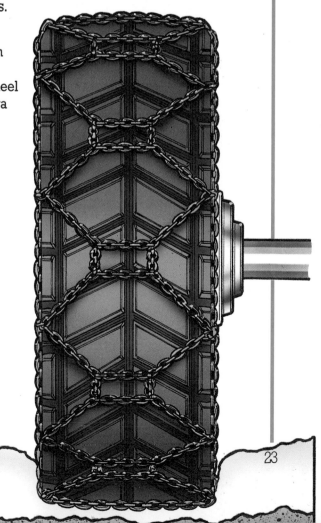

SPECIAL TRUCKS

Some jobs require specially designed trucks. Firefighting trucks have to carry their own water supply and need powerful pumps to shoot out the water at high pressure through hoses. Fire trucks used at airports spray foam instead of water to fight aviation fuel fires. The foam prevents air reaching the fuel.

Concrete mixers need a special type of container to carry wet concrete to building sites. The container on the back of the truck is rotated by a link to the engine. The continual movement of the container is essential to prevent the concrete from hardening before it reaches its destination. If a concrete

These fire trucks have stabilizing arms at the rear so that the turntable ladders remain steady.

mixer should break down or run out of fuel and not be able to keep its engine running, the load of concrete would very quickly begin to harden.

Crane transporters are usually very low and flat, so that a crane can lie along the top of them. They need hydraulic systems to raise and lower the crane.

A crane-carrying truck.

Before the crane is raised, sturdy steel legs must be extended to the ground on either side of the vehicle to keep it from toppling over.

In the United States, vehicles similar to crane transporters are specially designed to carry and operate oil drilling equipment.

Construction vehicles and other specialized trucks often use hydraulic rams. These are pistons forced to extend by pumping high pressure oil against them. They are very powerful, and can be used to move or support great weights.

Car transporters use hydraulic rams to raise and lower the top deck when loading and unloading. Garbage trucks use them to compress trash into a much smaller space so that they can collect more on each round. Dump trucks unload by using a hydraulic ram to tip up one end of the load container. The loose load slides out of the opposite end. Low-loading trailers use rams to support the heavy objects they carry.

A Bedford Afghan truck decorated by its driver.

SPORTING TRUCKS

Custom trucks originated in the United States among drivers who owned their trucks. They tried to make their trucks look different from all the others on the road by painting them with startling designs and pictures. Customization may also include replacing some of the standard parts of a truck, such as the exhaust "stack" (a vertical exhaust pipe), and the fuel tank, with highly polished chromium plated parts. The demand for customized trucks is so great in the United States that many manufacturers now supply their trucks in a range of different color schemes. These serve as a starting point for the owner's unique "paint job."

Articulated truck tractors are mostly used to pull especially heavy loads along public highways at normal speeds, but the powerful tractors without their trailers are capable of traveling at very high speeds. Truck racing is one of the fastest growing motor sports in Europe.

Trucks have also taken part in ordinary car rallies including the annual Paris-Dakar race.

A truck "Superprix" race at the Brands Hatch circuit in England.

Truck racing using truck tractor units started in the United States, and then rapidly spread to Europe. There is now a European Truck Racing Championship. Every year, professional racing teams supported by many of the truck manufacturers compete for the title. The races test the trucks' top speeds and road-holding to the limit. The majority of the drivers still earn their living by driving ordinary trucks on the roads when they are not racing. Truck racing drivers do not yet receive the enormous amounts of money that Formula 1 racing drivers enjoy.

As with motor car racing, many of the improvements in ordinary truck design, engine efficiency and safety are made as a result of experimentation on the race-track.

A "funny car" with outsize wheels.

A Leyland Land train doing a "wheelie" at an exhibition event.

HISTORY OF TRUCKS

The first self-powered vehicles used to transport goods and freight in the 19th century were driven by steam engines. The steam engine was unreliable, and steam powered trucks were not very successful.

The gasoline-fueled internal combustion engine, developed by the two German engineers Gottlieb Daimler and Karl Benz in 1887, provided a much cleaner and more reliable source of power for all types of vehicles. Daimler built the first motor truck (1896).

A 1911 British Lacre 2-ton lorry.

Although horses were widely used to transport supplies during World War I (1914-1918), motor trucks were also used in large numbers. After the war, they began to take over from horses as a means of transporting goods. They were powered by gasoline engines and this remained the most common type of truck engine until the 1930s. During World War II (1939-1945), the heavy oil engine, invented by Rudolf Diesel in 1897, began to increase in popularity.

Soon after its invention, the heavy oil engine became known as the diesel engine. It became more popular because it was more economical than the gasoline engine.

The Chevrolet 1-toner, 1926.

Diesel trucks developed more quickly in Europe than in the United States because the US had its own supplies of cheap gasoline. Gasoline engines remained popular there until the 1960s, when rising imports of more expensive oil made diesel trucks more attractive.

Throughout Europe, the majority of trucks have had diesel engines since World War II.

A 1931 Chevrolet pickup truck.

Until the 1950s, truck driving needed great physical strength. The steering wheel was hard to turn, especially when the truck was fully loaded, because of the great weight pressing the tires onto the road. Power-assisted steering made trucks easier to control. Bigger and heavier trucks, with two steering axles instead of one, could be built.

A modern articulated truck with freezer.

In the 1950s, Swedish manufacturers found that a turbocharger could boost a diesel engine's power output by up to 50 percent. Since the 1950s, articulated trucks have become very popular. Most are cab-over models, where the whole driver's cab tilts forward to reveal the engine for inspection and repairs.

In the late 1960s, truck designers tried a new type of engine, the gas turbine. It was unsuccessful because of high fuel costs. Freight transportation changed dramatically in the 1970s with the adoption of standard size containers. Trucks are now becoming more aerodynamic, using their shape to reduce air resistance and, therefore, fuel costs.

Facts and figures

The world's most powerful truck is a 1987 Ford LTL 9000. The truck, which weighs 4.4 tons, has reached a speed of more than 338 kph (210 mph) over a 400 meter (1,312 feet) track from a standing start.

The biggest transportation vehicles ever constructed are the two Marion crawler-transporters used to carry Apollo-Saturn 5 rockets, and now Space Shuttles, to their launch pad. Each crawler weighs 2,721 tons unloaded and 8,165 tons fully loaded with a Space Shuttle sitting on top on its mobile launcher platform. The crawler's maximum unloaded speed is 3.2 kph (2 mph). When loaded, it travels at 1.6 kph (1 mph).

The world's most powerful fire engine is the Oshkosh airport pumper. It weighs 60 tons and can spray 190,000 liters (over 40,000 gallons) of foam in 2½ minutes.

The world's largest tires are those used for for dump trucks. They each measure 3.65 meters (12 feet) in diameter and weigh 5.6 tons (12,500 pounds).

The largest dump truck in the world is the Titan 33-19, built by the Terex Division of General Motors. The giant vehicle stands 17 meters (56 feet) high when tipping and weighs 548.6 tons when fully loaded. It is so big that it cannot be driven on the roads. It is carried to its workplace in pieces and constructed there.

GLOSSARY

Articulated truck
A truck constructed in two parts – a tractor unit and a semitrailer.

Chassis
The basic framework of a truck to which everything else is attached. The engine and transmission may form part of the chassis.

Compressor
A turbine used to squeeze a gas (usually air) into a smaller space, and, therefore, increase its pressure.

CV
Cheval Vapeur, the French equivalent of HP, meaning horsepower. Both are measures of the power of driving force of an engine.

Diesel
The most common type of truck engine. It uses a heavy fuel oil, also called diesel or DERV.

Fifth wheel
The linkage that connects an articulated truck's tractor to its semitrailer.

GCW
Gross Combination Weight. The maximum permitted weight of an articulated truck with its semitrailer.

GTW
Gross Train Weight. The maximum permitted weight of a rigid truck that is pulling a trailer.

GVW
Gross Vehicle Weight. The maximum allowable weight of a rigid truck.

Horsepower (HP)
A unit of power used to measure the power output of an engine, based on the power of a horse. One horsepower is equivalent to about 746 watts of electrical power.

Internal combustion engine
Any engine in which the combustion (burning) occurs inside the engine – a truck's diesel engine, for example.

Jackknife
A lethal type of accident where the semitrailer of an articulated truck swings out to one side, and pulls the tractor around out of control.

Radio Determination Satellite System (RDSS)
A new type of satellite location system that uses a transmitter in the truck and satellites in space to show a truck's position on a screen.

Rig
A slang name for a truck, especially in the United States.

Semitrailer
A trailer with road wheels only at the rear, used to make up an articulated truck, with its front end resting on the fifth wheel at the rear of the tractor. Small parking wheels at the front can be

jacked down onto the road when a tractor is not connected.

Shock absorber
A device used to prevent a truck from bouncing up and down on its suspension on a bumpy road.

Tachograph
A device for recording a truck driver's hours and vehicle operations.

Tare weight
The weight of a truck without any load on board.

Truckie
The driver of a motor racing team's car transporter and usually also the person responsible for the supplies and the racing cars' spare parts.

Turbine
A rotating fan-like device that can either pump a liquid or a gas, or be driven around by a flow of liquid or gas. A turbocharger uses both – the exhaust turbine is driven by the flow of exhaust gases, and this drives the compressor turbine that pumps air into the engine.

Turbocharger
A device used to increase the power of an engine. It uses the jet of gases escaping from the engine's exhaust to power an air compressor, which then increases the air pressure inside the engine.

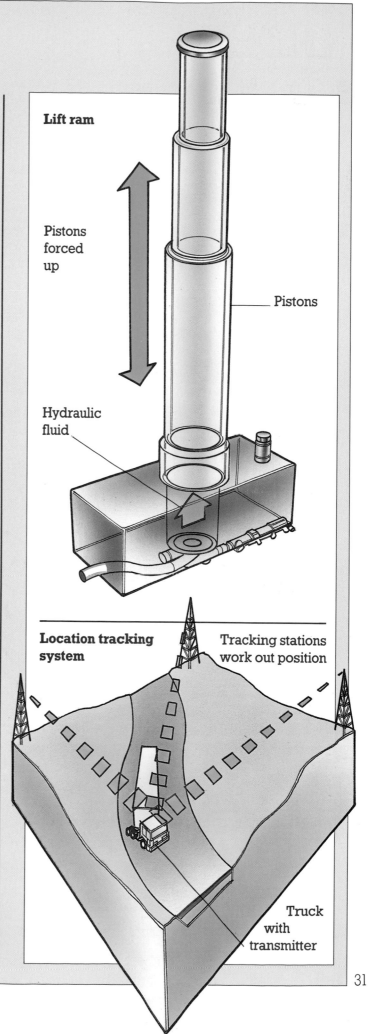

Lift ram

Pistons forced up

Pistons

Hydraulic fluid

Location tracking system

Tracking stations work out position

Truck with transmitter

INDEX

Photographic credits

Cover and page 7 top and middle: Spectrum; page 4: Ford Motor Company; pages 5 both, 16 top and middle, 17 bottom, 21, 23, 25, 26 and 27 top: Robert Harding Library; pages 6, 17 top, 20, 28 both and 29 bottom: Zefa; pages 7 bottom, 11, 12, 14 bottom, 16 bottom, 18 both, 19 bottom, 24, 27 middle and bottom and 29 top: Eye Ubiquitous; pages 14 top, 19 top and 22 top: J. Allan Cash Library; page 22: Frank Spooner Agency.